DESTINATION SPACE

MOON

David and Patricia Armentrout

A Crabtree Seedlings Book

Table of Contents

The Moon 4

The Surface of the Moon..8

Moon Phases..13

Men on the Moon...20

Glossary..23

Index..23

Moon

The Moon

After the Sun, the Moon is the easiest object for us to see in space. The Moon is more than one quarter of the size of Earth. It might appear close, but the Moon is about 238,855 miles (384,400 kilometers) from Earth.

Earth

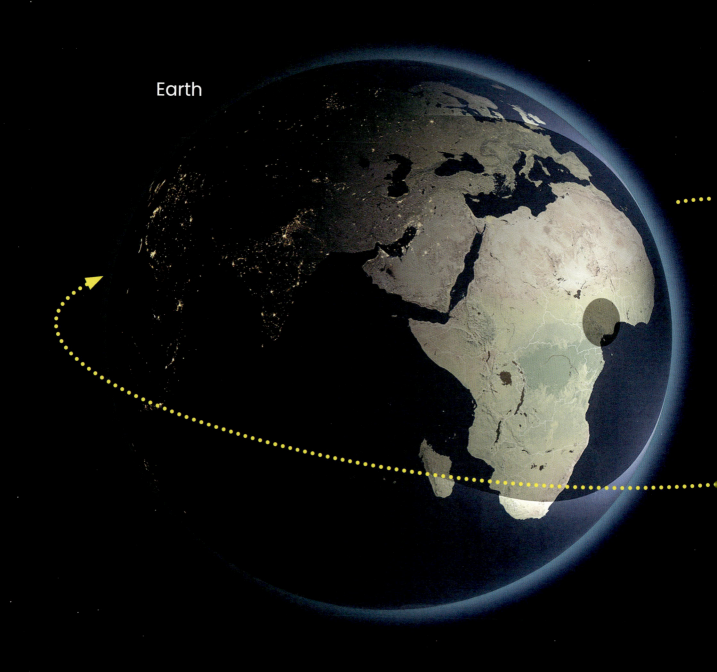

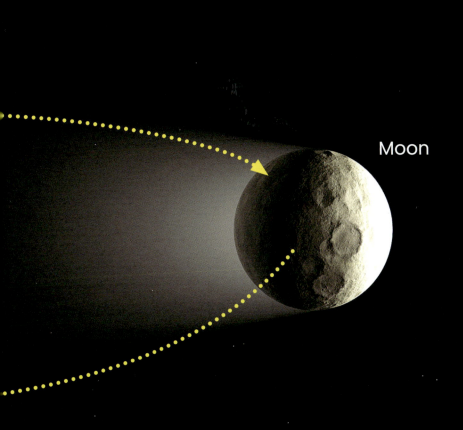

Moon

A satellite is an object that **orbits** or moves around a larger object. Earth is a satellite because it orbits the Sun. The Moon is a satellite because it orbits Earth.

The Surface of the Moon

The surface of the Moon is mostly rock and dust. The Moon's landscape includes ancient volcanoes, mountains, and craters.

The temperature on the Moon can reach over 260 degrees Fahrenheit (127 degrees Celsius).

9

If you throw a ball up into the air, what happens? The ball goes up and then falls to the ground. The force that brings the ball back down is **gravity**. Gravity gives us weight and holds us to the ground.

How much would you weigh on the Moon? The Moon's gravity is much weaker than Earth's. If you weigh 100 pounds (45.35 kilograms) on Earth, you would weigh only about 16.5 pounds (7.5 kilograms) on the Moon.

Moon Phases

The Moon seems to change every night. Sometimes it shines brightly in the night sky. Sometimes it's not visible at all.

The Moon shines because it reflects light from the Sun. As the positions of Earth and the Moon change, so does the portion of the Moon we see.

Scientists call these changes Moon phases.

During the **New Moon** phase, we can't see the Moon. The Moon gradually becomes visible as it moves through its phases.

The Moon is at Full Moon phase when it appears bright and round.

The Moon orbits Earth in just over 27 days, but it takes about 29.5 days to go through its phases.

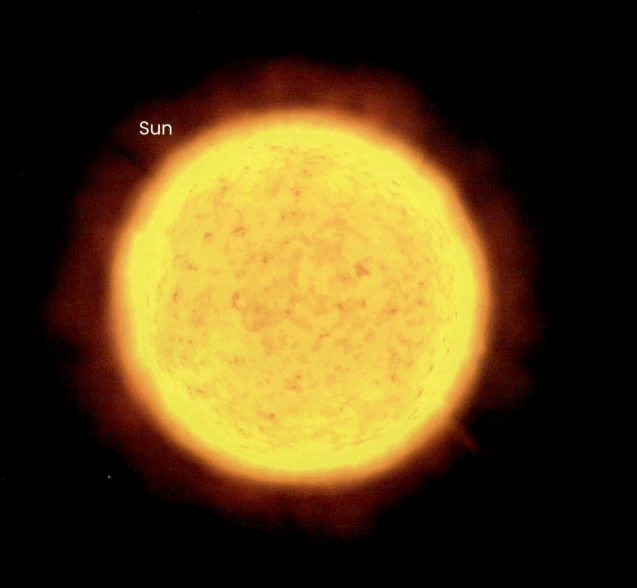

Only one side of the Moon can be seen from Earth. The side we don't see is sometimes called the dark side of the Moon.

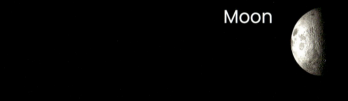

Apollo was a **NASA** space flight program. **Astronauts** made 11 *Apollo* space flights. In 1969, *Apollo 11* commander Neil Armstrong became the first person to walk on the Moon.

Armstrong's famous words after stepping onto the Moon were, *"That's one small step for (a) man; one giant leap for mankind."*

NASA's last flight to the Moon was the *Apollo 17* mission in 1972. NASA is now working on a new space flight program named *Orion*.

Orion

Orion's mission is to take astronauts back to the Moon and beyond in the coming years.

Glossary

astronauts (AS-struh-nots): People trained for space flight.

gravity (GRAV-uh-tee): A force that pulls and holds objects toward another object.

NASA (NASA): Short for National Aeronautics and Space Administration. A branch of the government responsible for the research and exploration of space and space travel.

New Moon (NOO MOON): When we cannot see the Moon lit by sunlight because it is between Earth and the Sun.

orbits (OR-bits): To travel in an invisible path around a larger object, such as a planet or a star.

Index

astronauts   20, 22
gravity   10
Moon phase(s)   13, 15, 17
NASA   20, 22

orbits   7, 17
satellite   7
Sun   4, 7, 14, 18

School-to-Home Support for Caregivers and Teachers

This book helps children grow by letting them practice reading. Here are a few guiding questions to help the reader build his or her comprehension skills. Possible answers appear here in red.

Before Reading

- **What do I think this book is about?** I think this book is about Earth's Moon. I think this book is about the different phases of the Moon.

- **What do I want to learn about this topic?** I want to learn about why we don't see a full Moon every night. I want to learn about the astronauts' trips to the Moon.

During Reading

- **I wonder why...** I wonder why we can't see the Moon every single night. I wonder why NASA sent astronauts to the Moon.

- **What have I learned so far?** I have learned that gravity is a force that pulls and holds objects toward another object. I have learned that Neil Armstrong became the first person to walk on the Moon.

After Reading

- **What details did I learn about this topic?** I have learned that Neil Armstrong's words after stepping onto the Moon were, "That's one small step for (a) man; one giant leap for mankind." I have learned that it takes just over 27 days for the Moon to orbit Earth.

- **Read the book again and look for the glossary words.** I see the word *orbits* on page 7, and the word *gravity* on page 10. The other glossary words are found on page 23.

Library and Archives Canada Cataloguing in Publication

CIP available at Library and Archives Canada

Library of Congress Cataloging-in-Publication Data

CIP available at Library of Congress

Crabtree Publishing Company
www.crabtreebooks.com   1–800–387–7650

Written by: David and Patricia Armentrout
Production coordinator and Prepress technician: Tammy McGarr
Print coordinator: Katherine Berti

Print book version produced jointly with Blue Door Education in 2022

Printed in the U.S.A./CG20210915/012022

Content produced and published by Blue Door Education, Melbourne Beach FL USA. This title Copyright Blue Door Education. All rights reserved. No part of this book may be reproduced or utilized in any form or by any means, electronic or mechanical including photocopying, recording, or by any information storage and retrieval system without permission in writing from the publisher.

PHOTO CREDITS:
Cover ©Juergen Faelchle; Page 2 © Castleski , Page 4-5 ©Dima Ze; page 6-7 ©Naeblys; page 8-9 ©Nostalgia for Infinity; page 10-11 © melis; page 12-13 ©Mr.Suchat; page 14-15 ©Juergen Faelchle; page 16-17 © robert_s; page 18-19 ©sebikus; All photos from Shutterstock.com except page 20-21 courtesy of NASA

Published in the United States
Crabtree Publishing
347 Fifth Ave.
Suite 1402-145
New York, NY 10016

Published in Canada
Crabtree Publishing
616 Welland Ave.
St. Catharines, Ontario
L2M 5V6